Creative Careers

Chef

Helen Mason

Gareth Stevens
PUBLISHING

Please visit our website, **www.garethstevens.com**. For a free color catalog of all our high-quality books, call toll free 1-800-542-2595 or fax 1-877-542-2596.

Library of Congress Cataloging-in-Publication Data

Mason, Helen.
Chef / by Helen Mason.
p. cm. — (Creative careers)
Includes index.
ISBN 978-1-4824-1298-7 (pbk.)
ISBN 978-1-4824-1187-4 (6-pack)
ISBN 978-1-4824-1475-2 (library binding)
1. Cooks — Vocational guidance — Juvenile literature. 2. Cooks — Juvenile literature. 3. Cooking — Juvenile literature. I. Mason, Helen, 1950-. II. Title.
TX652.5 M37 2015
641.5092—d23

First Edition

Published in 2015 by
Gareth Stevens Publishing
111 East 14th Street, Suite 349
New York, NY 10003

Developed and produced for Gareth Stevens Publishing by BlueApple *Works* Inc.
Editor: Marcia Abramson
Art Director: Melissa McClellan
Designer: Joshua Avramson

Photo Credits: Daniel et Daniel Catering and Event Creation: p. 13 top, 17 right, 39 top; Dreamstime: © Yap Kee Chan p.9; © Elitravo p. 10; © Tyler Olson p. 11 left; © Anna Baburkina p. 11 right; © Angelo Gilardelli p. 12; © Myroslav Prylypko p. 13; © Monkey Business Images p. 14, 30 bottom, 34; © Valentin Armianu p. 15; © Stephanie Frey p. 19; © Wavebreakmedia Ltd p. 22; © Ron Chapple p. 25 bottom; © Photographerlondon p. 26; © Ericro p. 28 top; © Duskbabe p. 28 bottom; © Gvictoria p. 29 top; © Hongqi Zhang p. 30 top, 36 top; © Zhukovsky p. 36; © Erwin Purnomo Sidi p. 37; © Konstantinos Papaioannou p. 38; © Algirdas p. 40 right; © Junkgirl p. 42; © Gavril Margittai p. 43; © Rmarmion p. 44 top; © Nastya22 p. 44; © Leonid Sadofev p. 45; © Helen Mason p. 9 top; © J. Avramson p. 27; Public Domain: p. 15 top, 42 top; p. 43 top; Shutterstock: © bikeri- derlondon cover, p. 5 top; © TaraPatta cover top right; © Jacques PALUT cover bottom right; © Arena Creative cover top left; © svry cover bottom left; © wavebreakmedia title p., p. 5, 6 top, 7, 8, 20 top, 21, 24, 29; © Tonis Valing TOC background; © sam100 TOC; © Hunterann p. 4 left; © Odua Images p. 4 right; © jesadaphorn yellow note paper; © kurhan p. 6 middle; © Tyler Olson p. 6 left; D7inami7s bottom p. 6, 22, 40; © Mr. Teerasak Khemngern p. 16; © Sergey Ryzhov p. 17 left; © Kondor83 p. 18; © Jeff Whyte p. 20; © Rido p. 23; © Stephen Coburn p. 25 top; © racorn p. 26 top; © bonchan p. 27 top; © Schweinepriester p. 31; Kondor83 p. 32 top; © Lucarelli Temistocle p. 32 bottom; © Pavel L Photo and Video p. 33; © Goodluz p. 35; © stockcreations p. 39 bottom; © Mr Pics p. 40 middle; © kai hecker p. 41 left; © s_bukley p. 41 right; U.S. Air Force photo/Airman 1st Class Katrina Heikkinen p. 15 top; Wikkicommons: © David Sifry p. 40 top

Manufactured in the United States of America

CPSIA compliance information: Batch #CS15GS. For further information contact Gareth Stevens, New York, New York at 1-800-542-2595.

Contents

What Is a Chef?

Many people know how to cook, but that doesn't make them chefs. The dictionary defines "chef" as a professional cook, which means that chefs are paid to cook.

Do you like food to look and taste good? Do you enjoy reading recipe books? Do you appreciate different flavors and like experimenting with ways to combine them? If you answered yes to any of these questions, you may make a wonderful chef.

A Kitchen Leader

Chefs are the leaders in the kitchen. They create menus, teach new recipes, and supervise all the workers.

▼ Chefs often taste a small sample of what they're cooking, and then adjust the flavors until everything tastes just right.

▲ Chefs must know how to cook many different dishes, often at the same time.

A Team Player

Although they are leaders, chefs also must be team players who work well with all the staff, including **apprentices** and dishwashers.

A Communicator

Chefs have to be good communicators. They need to talk to the owner about new dishes and order all the food ingredients. They also need to settle any disagreements between workers.

▲ The chef is also responsible for making sure that the kitchen is spotless.

◀ It's the chef's job to train other kitchen staff.

Types of Chefs

All chefs do some cooking, but some do more than others. Small **establishments** have only one chef. In that case, the chef manages the kitchen and cooks, too.

Large places may have one or more teams of chefs. The team captain is the executive chef.

▲ *Vegetable chefs prepare hot appetizers. They often make soups, pastas, and starches, as well as vegetable dishes.*

Executive Chef

Executive chefs are often so busy that they don't have time to cook, but they do create new dishes. They hire and train the staff to make sure their ideas are carried out successfully.

◀ *The executive chef plans menus, cooks special items, and makes sure everyone works together.*

Sous Chef

The sous chef is second-in-command. "Sous chef" means "under chef" in French. They take charge when the executive chef is out of the kitchen. They cook a lot, too.

Line Chefs

The other chefs in the kitchen are called line chefs. They work on the cooking line, assembling the different parts of each meal. Depending on the size of the kitchen, there may be a number of line chefs, each one with a specific job.

○ The fish chef prepares the fish dishes.
○ The roast chef roasts and braises meat. They also create any sauce that goes with the meat dish.
○ The pastry chef makes the baked goods, pastries, and desserts.
○ The cold-foods chef makes the salads, cold appetizers, and pâtés.

▼ In large kitchens, each line chef supervises a number of cooks and assistants.

7

Restaurant Chefs

Restaurants can be anything from casual to **gourmet**. Every restaurant needs chefs to plan menus and prepare and cook the food.

Fine Dining

Some restaurants specialize in gourmet dining. These places are formal. Each table has a tablecloth, centerpiece, china plates, and good silver. Service is slower. Chefs spend more time cooking. In fine dining, the

▲ *Chefs must work very quickly and coordinate with the other chefs so a table gets their many courses in the correct order.*

chefs are very creative and come up with different takes on common dishes. They present each dish so that it looks as good as it tastes. People often go to gourmet restaurants when they are celebrating an event such as a birthday, graduation, or wedding anniversary. They want the food to be as special as the occasion! It's also customary to wear nice clothes for fine dining. Leave the jeans, T-shirts, and flip-flops at home!

Casual Style Dining

Casual dining is a favorite of families. It's less formal than fine dining, but still has food served by waiters. The prices are more moderate. Some casual restaurants are part of national chains. Others are independent and may be owned by a family.

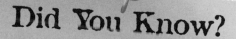
Ethnic Restaurants

Ethnic restaurants feature foods of different nationalities or cultures. Have you tried Chinese, Mexican, Italian, Thai, Japanese, Indian, Lebanese, or Ethiopian **cuisine**? All are a great way to sample food from another culture.

▲ In fancier restaurants, chefs often put their cooking skills on display. **Flambé** presentation is always popular.

◀ **Sushi**, which is raw fish, is a delicious Japanese dish. Many Japanese restaurants offer this healthful cuisine.

Hotels, Resorts, and Spas

Hotels, resorts, and **spas** have overnight guests. Chefs in these places prepare breakfasts, lunches, dinners, and snacks. Since guests may stay for a week or more, chefs have to plan several different menus.

Hotel and Resort Chefs

Hotels need large kitchens with many chefs because there is a lot of work to do, from supplying the restaurants in the hotel to catering special events and filling orders for room service. Hotel chefs must be ready for anything! One morning, they may serve breakfast to 100 writers, each with a different demand. Next, they may pack 300 lunches for a group of bikers. Then, they may cook for a wedding with 400 guests.

▶ Resorts often have **buffets**. This chef is preparing a fresh crepe as the guest waits.

Spas

People visit a spa when they want to improve their health and beauty. Guests usually start their stay by talking to the executive chef about their health needs. The chef then makes up special meals to suit those needs.

Many spas serve organic food. They buy fruit and vegetables that have been grown without chemical fertilizers and meat that has been raised without using **hormones** to speed the animals' growth.

▼ This spa chef grows fresh herbs to add a special flavor to the menu.

▲ This waiter is letting a chef know about a guest's food allergies. The chef will prepare this guest's food very carefully. Someone with a peanut allergy cannot eat peanuts or anything fried in peanut oil.

Catering Chefs

Catering companies prepare meals for special events, such as weddings, bar and bat mitzvahs, and corporate gatherings. Chefs plan the food for the event.

Planning Ahead

Plans start long before the date. The chef first meets with the client to find out what they want.

- Parents planning a surprise graduation party may want the chef to bake and decorate a cake.
- A family reunion may need 100 roast beef dinners.
- A chocolate convention may ask for 3,000 special desserts.

The chef estimates the amount of food, calculates a price, and then makes up a contract. The contract lists what the chef will cook, the cost, and when the customer will pay. If the catering company is a large one, an event planner meets with the clients, handles the contract, and coordinates with the chef.

Handling the Day

Food is usually made in advance and taken to an event, but some may be cooked onsite. Either way, chefs make sure the right ingredients, tools, and dishes get there.

Large caterers may have more than one event on the same day. Imagine taking care of a convention, family reunion, and graduation party all at the same time!

▲ *Presentation is very important at catered events. Everything must look beautiful.*

▼ *The kitchen for this wedding is in the open, outside the tent where the guests are served. There's a second plan in case of rain.*

Volume Cooking

Some chefs prepare meals for many people at the same time. Hospitals, nursing homes, schools, and colleges hire chefs to prepare meals for many people at the same time. This is called volume cooking.

Chefs in Schools

Chefs work in schools at all levels, from local elementary schools to colleges. They prepare fresh food in creative ways that appeal to young people. School meals also must be inexpensive so students and their families can afford them. To keep costs low, chefs buy the fruits and vegetables that are in season.

Chefs in Hospitals

Hospital chefs must make a variety of meals because patients often have special dietary needs. People on liquid diets, for example, need healthy broths, while other patients need food that works for their soft or low-salt diets. The meals need to tempt the patients and help them get well.

◀ *School lunches must do more than look good. Chefs follow US nutrition rules to make sure healthy choices are offered.*

Chefs in Nursing Homes

People in nursing homes and other senior residences may not see or hear very well, but many still look forward to good meals. Chefs research the needs of older people. They use foods such as oatmeal to help lower **cholesterol**, which can lead to heart problems.

▶ Some chefs also cook for Meals on Wheels. Volunteers bring the meals to people who can't shop for food and cook their own.

▼ **Grilled** fish is good for elderly people. Salmon provides **protein** and is a source of **omega-3s**.

Pastry Chefs

Is there a cake you remember? Maybe someone made a clown cake for your birthday party when you were younger, or your friend made cupcakes shaped like rabbits for Easter. Chefs who specialize in making desserts are called pastry chefs.

What They Do

Pastry chefs make fancy baked items. Some have jobs in bakeries, while others work in large restaurants that have their own pastry chefs. Wherever they work, pastry chefs measure and mix ingredients, shape and bake dough, and add fillings and decorations. What they create looks almost too good to eat.

For catered events, pastry chefs find out what the client wants and create special desserts.

◀ *Pastry chefs make cakes, candies French pastries, and more!*

Science and Sales

Baking takes a lot of chemistry. Baking powder, for example, makes cake rise. It takes just the right amount to get the proper result.

Yeast helps breads rise. Yeast must be kept warm or it will not grow.

Many pastry shops sell to both retail and **wholesale** customers. They bake desserts for large restaurants that sell them with meals. They also sell directly to the public.

▼ Decorating works of art takes patience. This pastry chef uses an icing bag and special tips to make tiny icing roses.

▲ Tiered cakes like the one pictured here are centerpieces at many weddings.

Research and Development Chefs

Research and development chefs work on improving or creating new products. They work for hotels, restaurant chains, and food manufacturers. Sometimes they will be asked to revise a current product so it has less sugar or fat.

Food Research

Some work with food companies. They look for ways to develop foods that can be **mass-produced**.

Suppose a company wants to make a new yogurt. Chefs research different ways that yogurt is made. They test different methods. As they work, they make notes. They will try to come up with a new flavor or style of yogurt that will stand out in the marketplace.

▶ Chefs look for new ways to make delicious food. How can they combine noodles with tomato sauce in a new way?

Other Research Jobs

Chefs also work in the test kitchens of magazines, newspapers, and websites. They make up and test recipes. As they're cooking, they write down exactly what they do and everything they use.

Groups of chefs taste the new dish and discuss how to improve it. They change one ingredient at a time until they like the taste. Chefs may also test the dish by serving it to a panel of readers who have volunteered to give their opinions.

▼ *Magazines are often planned around a theme. Chefs research what foods to cook for a season or holiday. They then develop new recipes, such as this elegant turkey.*

Working for Yourself

Some chefs start their own catering business, run a food truck, open a restaurant, or work as a personal chef.

Advantages and Disadvantages

Being your own boss is a great opportunity, but it can be stressful. You are responsible for everything and must work constantly. It's also important to have a positive attitude and lots of good ideas for growing the business. You also need a good location for your business, or you won't have enough customers.

▲ Many owners depend on kitchen staff to notice what needs doing — and to do it. They hire people who will go the extra mile.

▼ Food trucks can move around and always be in the best location. Many workers and walkers are looking for good fast food.

Personal Chef

Personal chefs work in their clients' homes to make lots of meals ahead of time. They find out what a family likes and whether there are special needs, such as a low-fat diet. Then they plan meals, buy ingredients, do the cooking, and pack everything up in the fridge or freezer for the client to eat later. The main difference between catering and being a personal chef is that the personal chef works in the client's home.

Private Chef

A private chef makes every meal every day for just one client. Many celebrities and sports stars have private chefs who work in their homes or even aboard their yachts.

▼ This caterer discusses the menu with a customer. Chefs who run their own business often do much more than cook.

Day in the Life of a Restaurant Chef

Being a restaurant chef means being busy from early in the morning until late in the evening. Here is what a typical schedule looks like for a restaurant chef. In a large restaurant, the chefs will share some of these jobs. In a family-owned restaurant, the owner-chef's spouse, children, siblings, and parents all may help out.

▲ This chef listens to a food distributor to find out more about specialty cheeses.

Before Noon

8:00 a.m. — Check local market for fresh produce and pick up the best. In some areas, chefs do this at 6:00 a.m.

9:00 a.m. — Arrive at the restaurant. Check what has been delivered. Make sure the food is fresh.

9:30 a.m. — Start the soup of the day. Prepare the day's meat.

10:30 a.m. — Direct the staff to make sauces, chop vegetables, and prepare garlic bread. Start desserts.

11:00 a.m. — Start cooking lunch. Coach staff.

After Noon

2:30 p.m. — Take a break. Start dinner. Order more food if needed.

3:30 p.m. — Order food for the next day. Pay the bills and check the budget. Write up the dinner specials.

4:30 p.m. — Coach the others in cooking the specials. Supervise as staff make dinner sauces, vegetables, and meat.

6:00 p.m. — Cook, taste, watch, help, compliment, and supervise. Make sure everyone is ready for evening service.

10:00 p.m. — Finalize the next day's menu and orders. You can't leave until everything is ready for the next day.

▶ In a small kitchen, the chef may prep the day's vegetables. Larger kitchens have prep cooks.

The Work

Chefs measure, mix, and cook ingredients. They turn fruits, vegetables, meat, and other staples into great meals.

Planning and Cooking

Chefs plan menus, calculate how much of each ingredient is needed, and then do the ordering. They also keep track of costs and monitor changes in food service laws.

The chef does some of the cooking and oversees the rest. No dish can be better than the rest. Everything must have the same high quality.

▼ *This chef is making sure the dishes to be served are in perfect order.*

Supervising

Chefs supervise the kitchen workers who prep the food. Food prep includes:

○ washing fruits and vegetables
○ storing any food that won't be used right away
○ getting ingredients ready to cook

While meals are being prepared, the chef is responsible for making sure everything is done right. If the recipe calls for 5 ounces of fish, each dish must have exactly that amount—no more, no less.

▲ *Many recipes need an exact amount of meat or fish. Chefs use a scale to weigh the right amount.*

Policing

Chefs are also the kitchen cops. They are responsible for making sure staff members follow food safety rules. All staff must keep themselves and their work areas spotlessly clean.

▶ *Hats like these are more than a symbol of honor. They keep hair in place and out of the food.*

Chef's Toolbox

Chefs use many different tools, such as tongs, spatulas, and scoops. Many are made from stainless steel because it is easy to clean and lasts a long time.

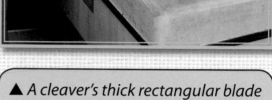

Knives

A knife is more than a tool. It is an extension of the chef's hands.

▲ A cleaver's thick rectangular blade is heavy enough to cut through bone.

Chefs handle, sharpen, and clean them with care.

A chef's kit includes many different knives. There is a special knife or cleaver for cutting through bones, one for separating meat from bone, and another for **filleting** fish. There's a short knife for paring and trimming vegetables, and another for slicing cooked meat.

▼ This chef's kit includes knives and a knife sharpener.

Mandoline

A mandoline slices vegetables into different thicknesses. It also makes fancy cuts such as juliennes, which are short, thin strips.

Food Processor

Food processors chop and mix foods. Chefs use them to make salads, soups, and sauces. Processors are great for **purées**. To make one, chefs start with a pea, bean, potato, or squash soup. They **process** the soup into a thick mixture without lumps.

Did You Know?

A set of good chef's knives can cost more than $1,000! Many chefs make this investment at the beginning of their careers. The knives last a lifetime.

▼ Mandolines cut vegetables in various fancy ways. Some shapes make the vegetables easier to cook. Others add to the visual appeal of the dish.

▲ A food processor can quickly turn chunky vegetable soup into a purée. Puréed soups can be eaten hot or cold. They are often used as appetizers.

27

Kitchen Skills

Here are some of the most important skills chefs need to learn.

Chopping

Chopping refers to cutting food into chunks. The food is cleaned and peeled first. Then the chef cuts it into pieces that are about the same size.

▲ *The tip of the knife should never leave the cutting board. This allows more control when cutting.*

▲ *Chefs keep their fingers away from the knife blade. They make a claw with the hand holding the vegetable, tucking away the tips of their fingers.*

Cutting

To cut, chefs wrap their index finger around the knife handle. Their thumb runs along the top of the opposite side. The other fingers curl around the handle. This position keeps the knife stable. Chefs can use it to make finer cuts.

The chef's other hand holds the object being cut. The thumb is against its back edge. The fingers are curled away from the knife blade.

28

Measuring

Chefs prefer to weigh the amount of each ingredient. This is particularly important for baking.

They use measuring spoons for small amounts and measuring cups for liquids.

Whisking

A whisk is a metal tool with a long, thin handle and metal loops. Chefs use a fast circular motion to whisk. This adds air, making a fluffy mixture. Whisks are used in recipes with a lot of eggs and to remove lumps from gravy.

▲ Measuring equipment uses both US and metric measures. Thermometers give readings in both centigrade and Fahrenheit degrees.

◀ A chef uses a whisk to whip cream. It is important to start with clean and dry equipment. Moisture can stop the cream from whipping. So can contact with plastic.

Becoming a Chef?

Start at Home

Start in your own kitchen by helping to prepare meals. Carefully use a knife to cut fruits and vegetables. Learn how to peel. Play memory games. This will help you learn to focus.

Try some of the recipes. What do you like? What changes would you like to make? Experiment. Make notes about what you like best and why.

▲ *Baking gives experience in measuring, mixing, and rolling. You can eat your mistakes.*

Volunteer

Offer to help out at a community food bank or soup kitchen. Both places cook a lot of food. Many food banks also teach cooking. You can help and learn at the same time.

◄ *Volunteering can be both informative and very rewarding.*

Take a Cooking Class

Many community centers offer cooking classes for young chefs. Check with your local centers for more information.

In many areas, 4H, Girl Scouts, and Boy Scouts offer cooking clubs and badges. Some towns have cooking classes just for kids.

Interview a Chef

Make arrangements to talk to a chef, ask to follow one for a day, or invite one to talk to your class. What do they like about the job? What do they dislike? What tips do they have for getting started?

▲ There are lots of jobs in kitchens. Talk to a local chef. Many will offer a part-time job.

Work in a Kitchen

Start at the Bottom

Visit local restaurants. Ask about getting a job washing dishes or busing tables when you are old enough. Busing involves setting tables and clearing dishes and cutlery away when customers are finished. Carrying dishes will build muscles.

▲ *Working at a fast food outlet provides experience in using a deep fryer, cooking on a grill, and paying attention to cleanliness.*

When to Start

You will need to be at least 14 or even 16 to get a part-time job in a restaurant. Research your state laws to see when you can apply for jobs.

◀ *The path to the kitchen often starts in the dining room. Many young people get their first job busing tables.*

Observe and Inquire

Once you have a job, watch what the other workers are doing. Who works well?

Ask questions and listen to the answers. That will show that you're interested and want to learn.

Make a Good Impression

If someone is busy, offer to help. Try to learn the skills they are using. When someone calls in sick, offer to learn their job. Take notes.

By following these tips, many young chefs work up from dishwashing to food prep. They improve their knife skills and then start cooking.

Be willing to start with simple things, such as garlic bread. Chefs who see you can do that well may be willing to let you try something else.

▼ *If your family owns a restaurant, you are allowed to start helping out at an early age.*

Education

Chefs learn in different ways. Some work in kitchens before finishing high school. Others finish high school and go to culinary school. Still others study food science at a college or university.

High School

Chefs need good communication and math skills. Many learn these skills in high school. They take courses in:

- **Food prep and cooking**. Students learn by making dishes and tasting each other's creations.
- **Nutrition**. This helps chefs prepare healthy meals.
- **Computer skills**. Chefs use computers to do online research, make orders, and keep track of budgets.
- **Math**. A chef needs to know fractions and percentages for doubling and tripling recipes.
- **Business**. This helps a chef manage finances and personnel.
- **Science**. Chefs need to know how ingredients react to each other. They also must keep up with the latest scientific advances in cooking.

After High School

Graduates go to college to study cooking, baking, or restaurant management. They also may get hands-on experience in a training restaurant that is operated by the college and open to the public. At the end of their culinary-arts program, many are ready to become chefs themselves.

Culinary certification is offered by associations such as the American Culinary Federation. To become certified, chefs have to meet eligibility requirements and pass both a written and practical exam showing that they have the knowledge and skills to cook. They may have also apprenticed under a professional chef.

▼ *This apprentice receives coaching from a chef. Many chefs enjoy passing on their skills to others.*

Famous Cooking Schools

CIA

Many future chefs study at the Culinary Institute of America (CIA). The CIA started as a college in New York in 1946. There are now branches in California, Texas, and Singapore.

The college offers degrees in cooking, baking, and food sciences. Students can attend the college or study on their own. The CIA sells training manuals that prepare apprentices to take a certification exam.

Graduates become chefs, restaurant managers, food writers, and food stylists.

▲ Restaurants are eager to hire CIA graduates. Many have jobs before they finish.

▼ Chefs can improve their skills at the CIA's California campus. Chefs here focus on fresh ingredients, some of them grown on the school grounds.

Le Cordon Bleu

Le Cordon Bleu is an international cooking school with campuses in Europe, North and South America, Australia, and Asia. As the French name suggests, the school focuses on French cuisine.

Students can specialize in French cooking or pastry. Fast-track programs allow students to graduate within six to nine short months.

Restaurant owners prize chefs from this school. They love to brag that a Cordon Bleu chef is working in their kitchen.

They also may take pride in serving Cordon Bleu-style food, such as Chicken Cordon Bleu, which is a chicken cutlet stuffed with cheese, wrapped in ham, and fried.

▼ *Le Cordon Bleu teaches French cooking. French cooking is thought to be the best in the world.*

Related Careers

Many chefs have jobs related to cooking.

Writers

Some chefs write articles for food magazines or blogs, or start their own publication. They may write cookbooks or about the history of food.

▲ *Food travel writers travel and enjoy new food. They write about the experience for other travelers.*

Others become food critics. They visit restaurants and write about what they like and dislike.

Teachers

Some chefs work for schools that train chefs. They teach students what they need to learn in order to become a chef.

Some chefs teach amateur cooks how to prepare their favorite foods and try new recipes. These classes may be individual sessions or lessons for dozens of people. Other chefs open up special kitchens where they help people prepare batches of meals to take home and freeze.

Store Owners

Chefs also run groceries and delis. They sell gourmet food. They talk to customers about how to prepare and enjoy it. Some of these owners also give cooking lessons and cater.

Food Stylists

Food stylists prepare the food you see in ads, books, and magazines. They work with a photographer and a props person. Using spatulas, basters, picks, and paintbrushes, they make the food look so good that you want to take a bite.

▲ *This fine foods shop is owned and run by a chef. The chef makes and packages food. Customers buy it to enjoy and to share.*

◄ *Ice cream is hard to photograph because it melts under bright lights.*

Famous Chefs

Alice Waters

Alice Waters is an American chef, restaurant owner, author, and activist. She encourages people to cook with organic foods that are grown locally. Her work earned her the title, "Mother of American Food."

▲ Waters started the **Edible** Schoolyard, a project that has spread around the world.

Jamie Oliver

Jamie Oliver is a chef, author, and media star. He was born in England. Oliver encourages people to grow, cook, and enjoy food. To promote this, he has set up training kitchens where young people learn kitchen skills. He also promotes healthier food choices in school cafeterias.

▲ Oliver encourages the use of fresh, rather than processed, foods.

Rachael Ray

Rachael Ray is an American chef, TV personality, and author. She started out working at a candy counter. Later, she managed a hotel restaurant and then did the buying for a gourmet store. From listening to customers, she got interested in helping people learn how to cook simple meals.

Marcus Samuelsson

Marcus Samuelsson was born in Ethiopia. Today, he's a celebrity chef, restaurant owner, and author. His cooking uses ideas from his African and Swedish background. At 24, he was the youngest chef to ever receive a three-star restaurant review from *The New York Times*.

▼ *Ray specializes in recipes that take a short time to cook.*

▲ *Samuelsson was the guest chef for President Barack Obama's first state dinner. For that meal, he cooked with vegetables and herbs from the White House garden.*

41

Chefs Who Changed Cooking

Great chefs like Jamie Oliver and Alice Waters always learn from the master chefs who came before them. When you study cooking, you are sure to learn about these three famous chefs: James Beard, Auguste Escoffier, and Julia Child. Each one had a special style that continues to influence chefs today.

Auguste Escoffier

Auguste Escoffier was a famous French chef who lived from 1846 to 1935. He modernized French cooking. He also made cooking into a profession with the executive chef as boss, and introduced fancy dining rooms with lovely table settings.

▶ *Auguste Escoffier started working as an apprentice in his uncle's restaurant in the south of France when he was 13, then moved to Paris.*

James Beard

James Beard was a giant of a man who was one of TV's first celebrity cooks. He lived from 1903 to 1985. He helped develop American-style gourmet cooking, and his more than 20 cookbooks remain very popular today. His house in New York City has been made into an American culinary museum.

Julia Child

Julia Child got her start by showing how to make an omelette on TV! That 1962 show launched her career as an American food writer and TV personality who introduced French cooking to Americans. She was born in 1912 and died in 2004.

▶ Julia Child's TV kitchen is so famous, it has been put on display at the Smithsonian Museum of American History in Washington, D.C.

You Can Be a Chef

Now that you know so much about the career, do you still want to be a chef? Check out the following characteristics. Which traits do you have? Which ones are you developing?

▲ Art lessons in color and balance can help you make food look good.

I am
- ❑ artistic
- ❑ flexible
- ❑ organized
- ❑ hardworking

I enjoy
- ❑ working with my hands
- ❑ food
- ❑ cooking
- ❑ working with other people

If you have or are developing these traits, you might make a great chef.

▼ Try to be as creative as you can be when preparing meals for your family.

Set Your Goal

Decide what kind of chef you want to be. Research the needed training either online or by talking to a guidance counselor.

Find out the following information:

○ What high school credits do you need?

○ What schools offer the courses you want?

○ What do you need to get into those schools?

▲ *You can enter baking competions at school or at fairs. Practicing for these events is fun!*

Take Steps Now

Start today. Spend extra time on the subjects you need to become a chef.

Research local restaurants. When you are old enough, apply for an entry-level job in one of them. You could also try to get a summer job in a restaurant, snack bar, or camp kitchen.

Learn some kitchen skills. Put away money toward future chef training.

Make a record of the foods you cook. Develop a personal recipe file that explains where you got each recipe, how you changed it, and useful cooking tips. Take a picture of each dish.

Glossary

apprentice a person who learns a job or skill by working for a fixed period of time for a professional in a certain field

buffet food laid out so that diners can serve themselves

cholesterol a substance found in some foods that can cause serious health problems

cuisine a style of cooking

edible fit to be eaten

establishment a place of business

fillet a boneless slice of fish or meat

flambé to pour liquor over food and ignite it

franchise restaurants restaurants that are part of a larger chain

gourmet a word to describe fancy food or a person who especially likes fancy food

grill a metal framework used for cooking food over direct heat

hormone substance that affects how animals and plants function

mass-produced made in large amounts, usually by machines

minimum wage the lowest amount that can be paid to an hourly worker, by law

omega-3s a fatty substance found in fish that helps to lower cholesterol levels

process the steps needed to make a product. Processed foods are changed from their natural state.

protein a substance found in food that builds, maintains, and repairs tissues in your body

purées food prepared by cooking and straining or processing in a blender

spa a resort that specializes in helping people look and feel better

sushi rice and raw or cooked fish, served Japanese style

wholesale selling goods in large amounts at lower prices

For More Information

Books

Better Homes and Gardens, *New Junior Cookbook*. Hoboken, NJ: Wiley, 2012.

Oliver, Jamie. *Cook with Jamie: My Guide to Making You a Better Cook*. New York, NY: Hyperion, 2007.

Rosenbaum, Stephanie. *Williams-Sonoma Kids in the Kitchen: Fun Food*. New York, NY: Free Press, 2006.

Websites

American Culinary Federation (ACF)
www.acfchefs.org
This organization certifies chefs. Learn about the group, what it offers, and how it can help you.

Food Network
www.foodnetwork.ca/guides/kids/index.html
Get some great recipes you'll want to try.

Jamie Oliver
www.jamieshomecookingskills.com
Learn cooking skills from Jamie Oliver.

Publisher's note to educators and parents: Our editors have carefully reviewed these websites to ensure that they are suitable for students. Many websites change frequently, however, and we cannot guarantee that a site's future contents will continue to meet our high standards of quality and educational value. Be advised that students should be closely supervised whenever they access the Internet.

Index